SNOWFLAKE LAYETTE

LEISURE ARTS, INC. • Maumelle, Arkansas

LEARNING THE STITCHES

These garments use some stitches which may be new to you: the Double and Single Snowflake stitches, and the Cross Stitch. Before starting to work the garments, we suggest you make a practice swatch of each stitch to be sure you understand it, achieve even tension, and to check your gauge.

SNOWFLAKE STITCHES

The Double and Single Snowflake are both worked on a Foundation Row that differs from the usual method of starting with a chain of a specified length. On this Foundation Row, you start with only two chains, then add to the length as you work across. Even tension is important to the appearance of these stitches; you may feel a bit awkward as you work the first few rows, but relax, keep your work loose, and you'll soon develop a quick, even rhythm.

Foundation Row: Ch 2, pull up loop on hook to ½", YO loosely; insert hook into first ch from hook and pull up a ½" loop (3 loops now on hook, see ***Fig. 1***). YO, hold a ½" loop of yarn aside as in ***Fig. 2***.

*(**Note:** from now on, the process of holding this ½" loop of yarn aside will be abbreviated HBL, for **hold back loop**).*

Continuing to HBL, hook yarn and draw through all 3 loops on hook. Insert hook into held-back loop ***(Fig. 3)***, hook yarn and **loosely** draw through both held-back loop and loop on hook; release held-back loop: eyelet made; ch 1.

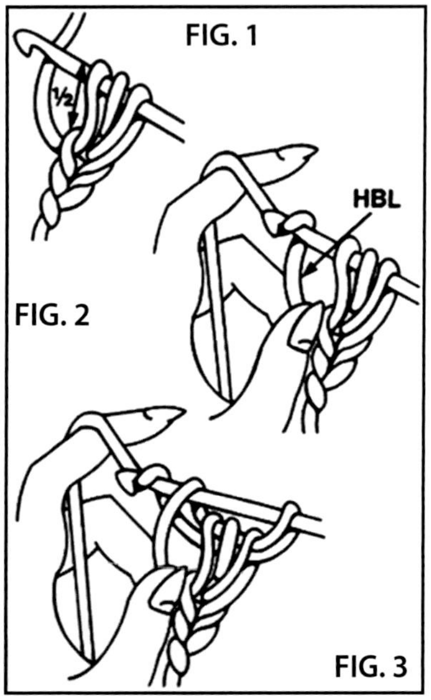

FIG. 1

FIG. 2

FIG. 3

*(**Note:** From now on, the process of inserting hook into held-back loop, hooking yarn and drawing loosely through both held-back loop and loop on hook, then releasing held-back loop, will be abbreviated **"form eyelet"**.)*

You have now completed one Snowflake leg. Compare your work with ***Fig. 4***, and find the space indicated "eyelet". This eyelet is important as you will be working into it to make the next leg, and into it again on the return row. Be sure not to confuse it with the space under the final ch 1. Your eyelet will not show up quite as clearly as in our diagram, where it is exaggerated for clarity. Find your eyelet now and remember these abbreviations:

HBL - Hold back a ½" loop of yarn ***(Fig. 2)***.

Form eyelet - Insert hook into held-back loop ***(Fig. 3)***, hook yarn and draw loosely through both held-back loop and loop on hook, release held-back loop.

FIG. 4

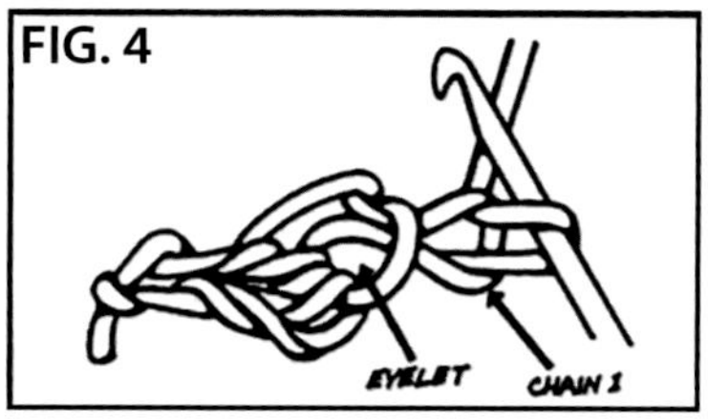

Now continue Foundation Row: ★ Pull up loop on hook to ½", YO, insert hook into eyelet of preceding leg, pull up a ½" loop as before (3 loops now on hook), YO, HBL, draw yarn through all 3 loops on hook; form eyelet; ch 1 loosely. Second Snowflake leg is now made.

Repeat from ★ **until you have as many legs as specified in pattern for Foundation Row**. For your practice piece, work a total of 10 legs. At end, do **not** turn.

SINGLE (7-LOOP) SNOWFLAKE PATTERN ROW

Work a Foundation Row as above as specified in pattern (for practice piece, this is 10 legs). Pull up loop on hook to ½".

*(**Note:** From now on, whenever pattern directs you to pull up a loop, that means pull it up to ½").*

YO loosely, insert hook into first eyelet to left and pull up a loop; (YO, insert hook into **next** eyelet and pull up a loop) twice: 7 loops now on hook ***(Fig. 5)***. YO, HBL, hook yarn and draw through all 7 loops on hook, continuing to HBL ***(Fig. 6, page 3)***; form eyelet, ch 1. ★ Pull up loop on hook, YO, insert hook into eyelet just underneath hook ***(Fig. 7, page 3)***, draw up a loop, YO and draw up a loop in next eyelet (this eyelet was used before), YO and draw up a loop in **next** eyelet (this eyelet was not used before): 7 loops now on hook. YO, HBL, hook yarn and draw through all 7 loops on hook. Form eyelet, ch 1 loosely. Rep from ★ across row.

FIG. 5

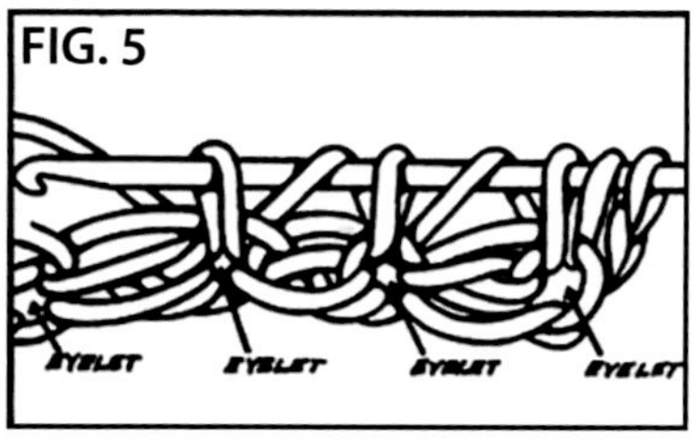

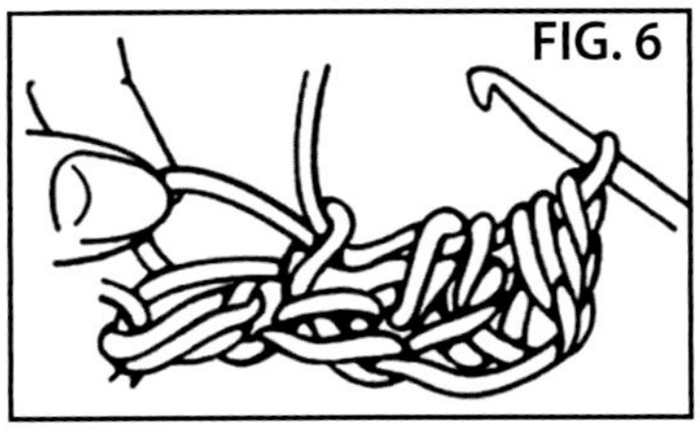

FIG. 6

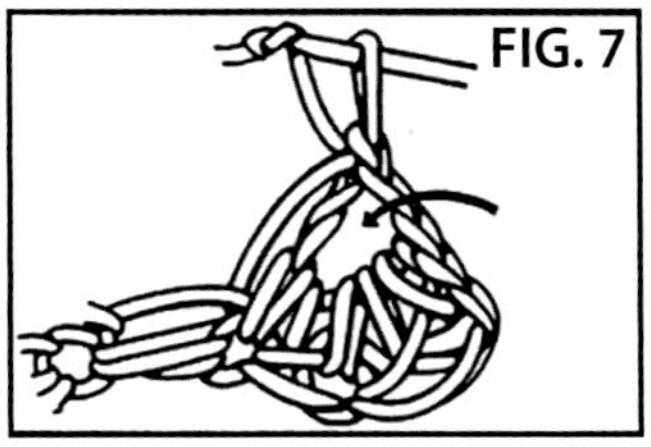

FIG. 7

*(**Note:** Be sure to work into the final unused chain (on first row) or eyelet (on subsequent rows) at the very end of row below, or you will make a decrease where you don't want one.)*

At the end of row, work one turning leg in eyelet just below hook as follows:

Turning Leg: Pull up loop on hook, YO loosely, insert hook into eyelet just below hook and pull up a loop: 3 loops now on hook. YO, HBL, hook yarn and draw yarn through all 3 loops on hook; form eyelet. Ch 1 loosely ***(Fig. 8)***, turn.

Rep Pattern Row from ★ for as many rows as desired. For practice piece, work 6 rows in pattern. Do **not** work turning leg at end of last row. Finish off.

DOUBLE (11-LOOP) SNOWFLAKE PATTERN ROW

Work a Foundation Row as above as specified in pattern (for practice piece, this is 10 legs). Pull up loop on hook, YO loosely, insert hook into first eyelet to left and pull up a loop; YO and pull up a loop in next eyelet (this eyelet was used before), YO and pull up another loop in same eyelet, YO and pull up a loop in the **next** eyelet, YO and pull up another loop in same eyelet: 11 loops now on hook ***(Fig. 9)***. YO, HBL, hook yarn and draw through all 11 loops on hook. Form eyelet, ch 1 loosely. ★ Pull up loop on hook, YO, insert hook into eyelet just underneath hook ***(Fig. 7)***, pull up a loop. (YO and pull up a loop in **next** eyelet, YO and pull up another loop in same eyelet) twice: 11 loops now on hook: YO, HBL, hook yarn and draw through all 11 loops on hook. Form eyelet, ch 1 loosely. Rep from ★ across row, making sure to work into very last chain **(beg ch of Foundation Row)** or eyelet (for subsequent rows) in row below. To turn, work one turning leg as for 7-Loop Snowflake in eyelet just below hook, turn. Rep Pattern Row from ★ for as many rows as desired. For practice piece, work 6 rows in pattern, do **not** work turning leg at end of last row. Finish off.

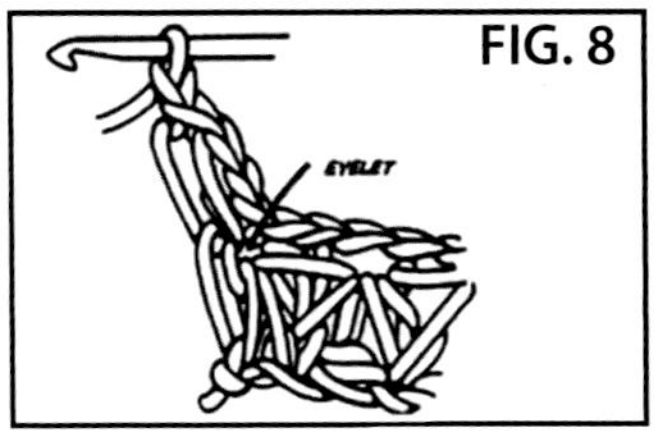

FIG. 8

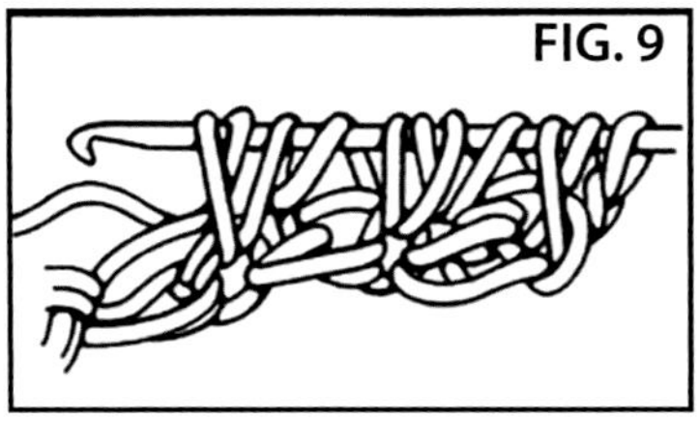

FIG. 9

Note: To work either Snowflake Stitch into an sc row instead of Foundation Row:
With right side of work facing, attach yarn with a sl st in sc at the upper right corner, pull up a ½" loop, work a turning leg in **same** sc. Work the Snowflake Stitch in usual manner, but use every other sc as an eyelet.

CROSS STITCH

This stitch is usually worked on a foundation of sc, using every other sc as you would use an eyelet in working the Snowflake Stitches. For practice swatch, ch 20, then work 2 rows sc before working pattern rows. At end of last row, do **not** chain, turn.

Pattern Row 1: Pull up loop on hook to ½". YO loosely, pull up a loop in first sc: 3 loops on hook; YO, HBL, hook yarn and draw through all 3 loops on hook. Form eyelet, ch 1. You have made a turning leg, and you have an eyelet just below hook. ★ Pull up loop on hook. YO and pull up a loop in eyelet just below hook, sk 1 sc, YO and pull up a loop in next sc, YO, pull up a loop in same sc: 7 loops on hook ***(Fig. 10)***. YO, HBL, hook yarn and draw through all 7 loops on hook; form eyelet, ch 1. Rep from ★ across. To turn, work 1 turning leg as for Snowflake Stitches, in eyelet just below hook, turn.

Pattern Row 2: ★ Pull up loop on hook, YO and pull up a loop in eyelet just below hook. Skip first eyelet on row below, YO and pull up a loop in next eyelet (Fig. 11). YO and pull up a loop in same eyelet; 7 loops on hook; YO, HBL, hook yarn and draw through all 7 loops on hook. Form eyelet, ch 1. Rep from ★ across. Work a turning leg as in Snowflake Stitches, turn.
For pattern, continue to rep Row 2 as many times as specified. For practice swatch, rep Row 2 twice **more**. At end of last row, do not work turning leg. Finish off.

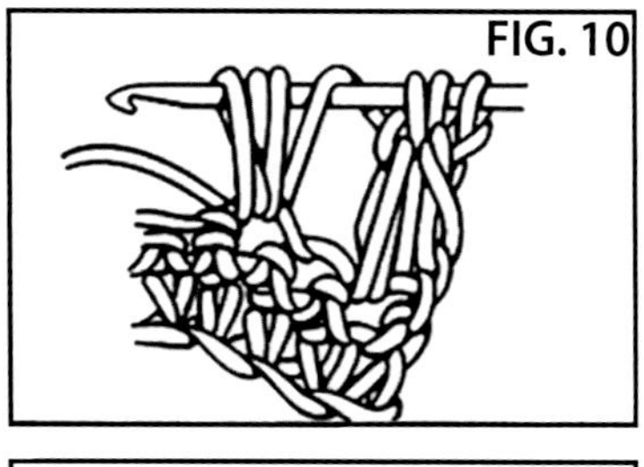

FIG. 10

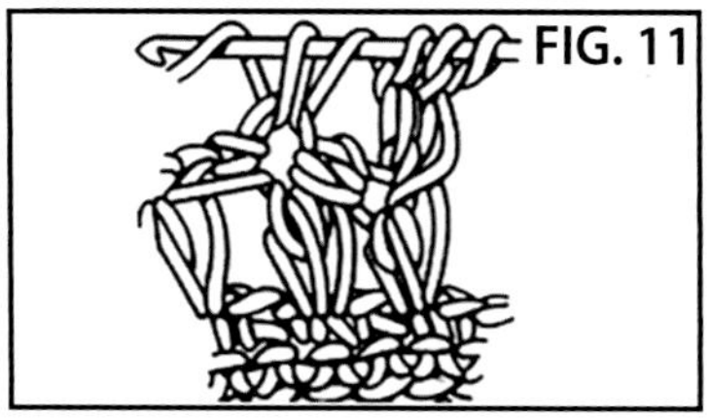

FIG. 11

LAYETTE

Garment Sizes:	**3 to 6 months**	**9 to 12 months**
Body chest	up to 18"	up to 19"
Sleeve length at underarm	6½"	7½"
Jacket length	9½"	11½"

Size Note: Instructions are written for smaller size with changes for larger size in braces.

MATERIALS (For Jacket, Booties and Hat)
Baby Weight yarn:
Blue - 5 ounces
White - 1 ounce
Size E crochet hook **or** size needed for gauge
¼" diameter Buttons - 3 (optional)

GAUGE: With E hook, in Foundation Row, 4 legs = 2"
In Snowflake Stitches, swatch of 10 legs and 6 rows should measure 5" wide and 3" deep

JACKET
BODY

Starting at bottom with Blue, make a Foundation Row of 43 legs.

Rows 1 thru 13{17}: Work 11-Loop Snowflake Pattern across row, remembering to work into very last chain (beg ch of Foundation Row) or eyelet (for subsequent rows), and to work a turning leg. Work until piece measures about 6{8}" **or** desired length to underarm; do **not** make turning leg at end of last row. Finish off Blue.

SLEEVE (Make 2)
Starting at cuff with Blue, make a Foundation Row of 19 legs. Being careful not to twist sts, form a ring by joining with a sl st to unused ch 1 at the beg of the Foundation Row.

Work 11-Loop Snowflake, starting with: pull up loop on hook to ½", YO, insert hook into joining ch, YO, pull up ½" loop (3 loops now on hook), YO, pull up a loop in next chain (this is 2nd ch of Foundation Row), YO, pull up another loop in same chain (YO, pull up a loop in next eyelet) twice; YO, HBL, hook yarn and draw through all 11 loops; continue to work 11-Loop Snowflakes around.

Join for next rnd by working an 11-Loop Snowflake using eyelet under hook, the ch you sl stitched into, and eyelet at very top of previous row: you should have 20 eyelets.

From now on, work continuously around without joining rnds. Continue in 11-Loop Snowflake pattern, working 11{13} rnds in all, until Sleeve measures about 5½ {6½}", **or** desired length to underarm. Finish off Blue.

Join Sleeves to Body
Row 1: Join White with an sc in eyelet at upper right corner of long side of Body. ★ Sc in top two strands of next leg, sc in next eyelet, rep from ★ until you have 19 sc for Right Front. Place one Sleeve on top of Body, with last round worked at top, and with jog of last round at inner center (***Fig. 12***).

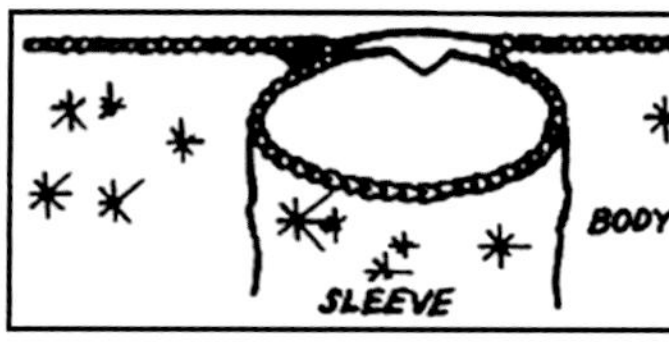

FIG. 12

With White, sc into closest Sleeve eyelet, ★ sc in top of next Sleeve leg, sc in next eyelet, rep from ★ until you have 30 sc across right Sleeve top, ending sc in leg. Skipping 5 legs and 4 eyelets of Body (these will later be sewn to back of Sleeve for underarm), continue with White in same manner working 1 sc in each leg and eyelet until there are 31 sc across back. Place second Sleeve on top of Body as before, work 30 sc across Sleeve top, skip 5 legs and 4 eyelets of Body for underarm, work 19 sc across Left Front. At this point you should have 129 sc. Ch 1, turn.

Row 2: Sc into back loop of each sc across. Finish off White.

YOKE (You will now work 2 rows of Cross Stitch)
Cross Stitch Row 1: Join Blue with a sl st through both loops of first sc at upper right hand corner of Right Front. Following Cross Stitch Pattern, work one leg into same sc, then work into every other sc 8 times (a total of 9 Cross Sts), across Right Front.

Decrease at Armhole: Pull up loop on hook, YO, draw up a loop in eyelet directly below hook (sk 1 sc, YO, draw up a loop in next sc) twice (7 loops on hook). YO, HBL, hook yarn and draw through all 7 loops on hook (dec made), form eyelet, ch 1. (Sk 1 sc, work a Cross St in next sc) 13 times across Sleeve. Work a dec as before in next 3 scs. Continue working a Cross St into every other sc across row, 13 Crosses across back, working decs at both points where Left Sleeve joins Body, as at Right Sleeve. Work turning leg, turn.

Row 2: Work 7 Cross Sts (turning leg does not count as a st throughout), dec, (work 12 Cross Sts, dec) 3 times, work 9 Cross Sts across Right Front. Break off Blue.

Row 3: Join White in first eyelet, sc in each eyelet and each leg across, ch 1, turn.

Row 4: Sc in back loop of each sc across. Break off White.

Row 5: Join Blue, ch 2, work 1 leg into first sc. Working Cross Sts and decs as in Row 1, work as follows across row: 7 Crosses, dec, (11 Crosses, dec) 3 times **more**, 8 Crosses across Left Front. Make turning leg, turn.

Row 6: Work 7 Crosses across Left Front, dec, 5 Crosses, dec (this dec is in the middle of the Sleeve), 3 Crosses, dec, 10 Crosses across back of Body, dec, 3 Crosses, dec, 5 Crosses, dec, 7 Crosses across Right Front. Break off Blue.

Rows 7-8: Join White, work as Rows 3 and 4, but do **not** break yarn, ch 4, turn.

Beading Row: ★ Sk 1 sc, dc in next sc, ch 1; rep from ★ across row, ending with dc in last st. Break off White.

Ruffle: With **right** side facing, join Blue in 3rd ch of ch-4 of Beading Row. Ch 4, dc in same st, work (1 sc, ch 3, 1 dc) in each dc across. Do **not** break yarn.

Left Front Edging

Row 1: Sc in side of each White sc at top of Left Front and in each leg and each eyelet down Front, ch 1, turn.

Row 2: Sc in each sc to top, ch 1, turn.

Row 3: Work ruffle edge as follows: (sc, ch 3, dc) in every other sc to bottom edge, work 2 ruffles in last eyelet at corner. Do **not** break yarn.

Lower Edge: Continue ruffle edge, working in eyelets only across bottom of Body; work two ruffles in last eyelet at corner. Do **not** break yarn.

Right Front Edging

Working up Front, rep Rows 1-3 of Left Front Edging, break yarn.

Finishing Sleeves

Rnd 1: With right side of work facing, at cuff join White, sc in each eyelet and each leg around, sl st to beg sc; ch 1, turn.

Rnd 2: Sc in back loop of each sc around, turn.

Rnd 3: Ch 4, ★ sk 1 sc, dc in next sc, ch 1; rep from ★ around, sl st to 3rd ch of beg ch. Break off White.

Rnd 4: Join Blue and work ruffle edging around. Sew Sleeves to Body underarms with backstitch. If desired, sew buttons on where White stripes at Yoke join the Front Edging. Ch-3 loops on edging serve as buttonholes.

Ties: With White, make a chain 36" long and 2 **more** chains each 15" long. Weave the shorter chains through the dc rows of each Sleeve, and long chain through dc row at neckline. Knot each end of each chain.

HAT

Wind Blue yarn around finger 4 times to form a ring ½" in diameter, slip ring off finger.

Rnd 1: Sl st into ring, pull up a ½" loop, work a turning leg into ring. Work as if you were making Cross Sts, but use ring as the eyelet, until you have 11 eyelets, join with a sl st to first eyelet, work a turning leg, but do **not** turn.

Rnd 2: Pull up a ½" loop, YO, pull up a loop in last eyelet formed, (YO, pull up a loop in first eyelet of previous rnd) twice: 7 loops on hook. HBL, YO and draw through 7 loops on hook (1 inc made). Make two 11-Loop Snowflakes. Continue around ring, alternating one inc Snowflake with two 11-Loop Snowflakes; do **not** ch 1 at end of last Snowflake: you should have 16 eyelets. Join with a sl st to first eyelet, work a turning leg.

Rnd 3: Rep Rnd 2; end by working last Snowflake Stitch in same sp as first st of rnd, do **not** ch 1 at end of last Snowflake: you should have 25 eyelets. Do **not** work turning leg.

Rnd 4: ★ Work three 11-Loop Snowflakes, one inc Snowflake; rep from ★ around; end by working last Snowflake and last inc in same sp as first st of rnd, do **not** ch 1 at end of last Snowflake. Join with a sl st to first eyelet. Work should be about 4½" in diameter with 32 eyelets on outside edge.

Rnd 5: Pull up a ½" loop, work a turning leg. ★ Work five 11-Loop Snowflakes, 1 inc Snowflake; rep from ★ 4 times **more**, finish off Blue.

The section of the hat with only 4 rnds of crochet becomes the back neck edge Do **not** work this edge until you work the edging.

FORM CROWN

Row 1: Join White with an sc in first eyelet of previous rnd. Sc in each eyelet and leg around; finish off.

Row 2: Join White in first sc of last row, sc in back loops of each sc across; finish off.

Row 3: Join Blue in first sc of previous row, pull up a ½" loop, work 1 leg in same sc, ★ sk 1 sc, work one Cross St in next sc; rep from ★ across row, work a turning leg in last eyelet, turn.

Row 4: Work 1 Cross St in each eyelet across to beg of previous row. **For large size only**, work 2 **more** rows in Cross St. Finish off.

Rows 5 and 6 {7 and 8}: Rep Rows 1 and 2.

Row 7{9}: Rep Row 3.

Row 8{10}: Repeat Row 4. Finish off Blue.

Row 9{11}: Join White at right-hand side of back neck edge, sc in each eyelet and leg around, join with a sl at in first sc; ch 1.

Row 10{12}: Sc in back of each sc to right front corner of hat.

Form 1st Tie: Ch 50, sc in 2nd ch and in each ch to corner. Sc in back loop of each sc across front edge of hat to left corner.

Form 2nd Tie: Ch 50, sc in 2nd ch and in each ch to corner. Sc in back loop of each sc, join with a sl st to first sc, finish off.

Front edging: Join Blue with a sl st in sc at right front corner of hat, just above tie. (Sc, ch 3, dc) in every other sc across front edge. Finish off.

BOOTIES (Make 2) (One size only)

SOLE

With White, make a Foundation Row of 7 legs.

Row 1: Work 11-Loop Snowflakes across row, remembering to work into ch at beg of previous row, and to work a turning leg.

Rows 2 and 3: Work as Row 1, do **not** work turning leg at end of Row 3, do **not** turn.

Row 4: Sc loosely into each eyelet and leg around all four sides of piece, join. Ch 1, turn.

Row 5: Sc in back loop of each sc around, join. Finish off White.

INSTEP

With Blue, make a Foundation Row of 3 legs.

Rows 1-3: Work 11-Loop Snowflakes across row, remembering to work into ch at beg of Foundation Row and to work a turning leg. At end of last row, do **not** turn.

Row 4: Sc loosely into each eyelet and leg around instep top.

Place instep at one end of Sole; with Blue, join by working sc into **back** loops of **both** pieces along one side, across toe, and up other side. Leave instep open ***(Fig. 13)***. Do **not** break yarn.

FIG. 13

CUFF

Rnd 1: Sc around Sole and into each sc across open edge of Instep; join to first sc with a sl st, ch 1.

Rnds 2-5: Sc around, join, ch 1. End last row, ch 4.

Rnd 6 (Beading)**:** ★ Sk 1 sc, dc in next sc, ch 1; rep from ★ around. Join with a sl st to 3rd chain of starting ch 4, ch 1.

Rnd 7: Sc in each sc and each dc around, join with a sl st.

Rnd 8: Pull up a ½" loop, work a Snowflake leg into same sc. Work 11-Loop Snowflakes into every other sc around; do **not** ch 1 at end of last Snowflake. Join with a sl st to first eyelet.

Rnd 9: Pull up a ½" loop, work a leg into first eyelet of previous row, continue around in 11-Loop Snowflakes; do **not** ch 1 at end of last Snowflake. Join with a sl st to first eyelet. Finish off Blue.

Rnd 10: Join White with a sl st; ch 1, sc in each leg and eyelet around, join with a sl st to beg ch 1.

Rnd 11: Ch 1, sc in each sc around, join with a sl st to beg ch 1. Finish off White.

Finishing: With Blue, work edging as for Hat.

With White, make a chain 14" long, weave through the dc row, and tie at front of Bootie.

CARRIAGE BLANKET

MATERIALS

Baby Weight yarn:
White - 8 ounces
Blue - 2 ounces

Size E crochet hook **or** size needed for gauge

GAUGE: With E hook, in Foundation Row, 4 legs = 2"
In Snowflake Stitches, swatch of 10 legs and 6 rows should measure 5" wide and 3"deep

Foundation Row: With White, work a Foundation Row of 71 legs.

Rows 1-8: Work in 7-Loop Snowflake Stitch.

Row 9: Work in 7-Loop Snowflake Stitch, but do **not** work turning leg at end of row. Finish off White.

Piece should measure about 4¼" deep and 35" wide.

Row 10: Join Blue with a sl st in eyelet at upper right corner. Sc in each eyelet and in each leg across, ch 1, turn.

Row 11: Sc in back loop of each sc across. Finish off Blue.

Row 12: Join White with a sl st through both loops of first sc, work across in Cross St, using every other sc.

Row 13: Work in Cross St, but do **not** make turning leg at end of row. Finish off White.

Rows 14 and 15: Repeat Rows 10 and 11.

Rep Rows 1 through 15, 3 times **more** (to start 7-Loop Snowflake in an sc row, see special instructions on page 2).

Rep Rows 1 through 9 once **more.**

You should now have 5 panels of 7-Loop Snowflake Stitch with 4 panels of Cross St separating them; piece should measure about 29½" x 34".

FINISHING

Steam blanket lightly, being careful not to flatten sts.

EDGING

Rnd 1: With White, sc in each leg and eyelet around, join with a sl st. Finish off White.

Rnd 2: Work ruffle edging as follows: join Blue with sl st, ★ (sc, ch 3, dc) in next sc, sk 2 sc. Rep from ★ for edging. Join with a sl st. Finish off Blue.

Rnd 3: With White, work ruffle edging around as in Rnd 2. Finish off White.

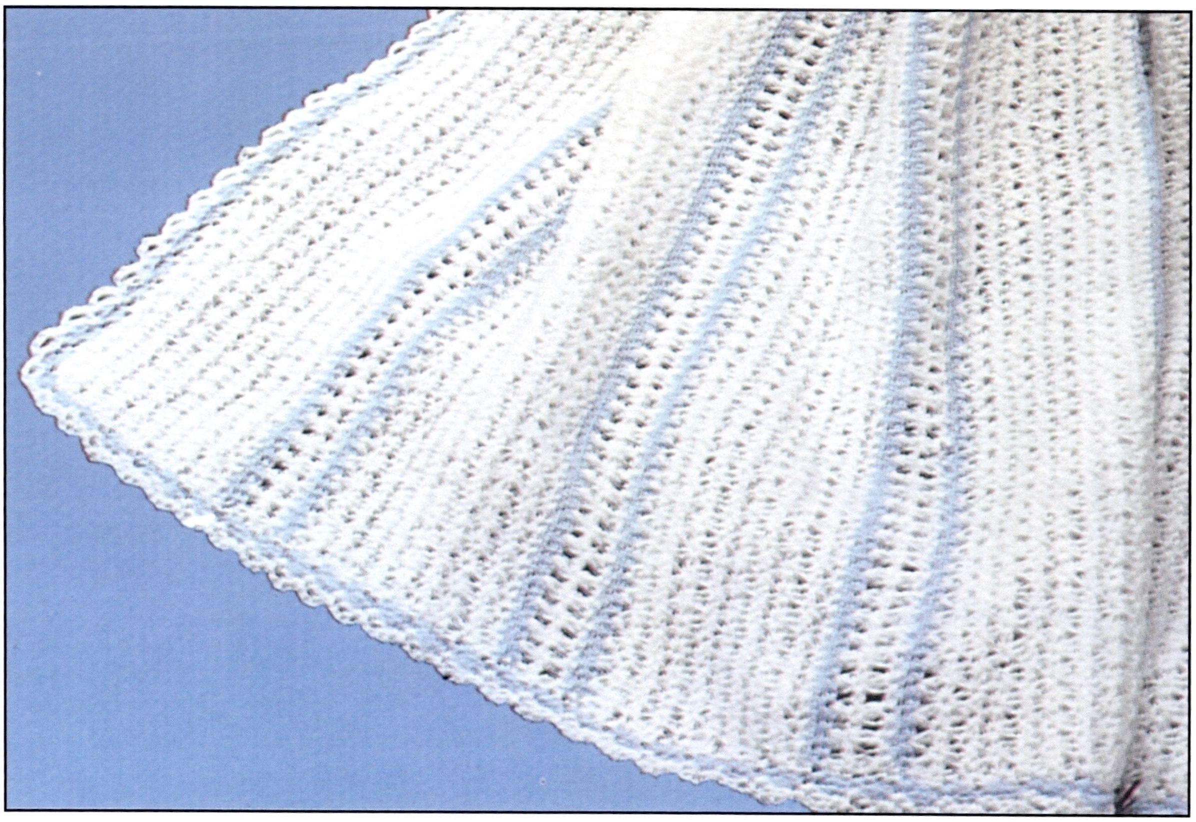

We have made every effort to ensure that these instructions are accurate and complete. We cannot, however, be responsible for human error, typographical mistakes, or variations in individual work.

Made in U.S.A.